NO LONGER PROPERTY OF
ANYTHINK LIBRARIES/
RANGEVIEW LIBRARY DISTRICT

Makers as
INNOVATORS
JUNIOR

Designing
Board Games

NO LONGER PROPERTY OF
ANYTHINK LIBRARIES /
RANGEVIEW LIBRARY DISTRICT

By Kristin Fontichiaro

CHERRY LAKE Publishing

Published in the United States of America by
Cherry Lake Publishing
Ann Arbor, Michigan
www.cherrylakepublishing.com

Series Adviser: Kristin Fontichiaro
Reading Adviser: Marla Conn, MS, Ed., Literacy specialist,
Read-Ability, Inc.
Photo Credits: Cover and pages 8, 10, 12, 18, and 20, courtesy of
Michigan Makers; page 4, TheUjulala / tinyurl.com/zglysvo / Creative
Commons CC0; page 6, tinyurl.com/guyd438; page 14, Ben Husmann /
tinyurl.com/gt3tfon / CC BY 2.0; page 16, Alexas_Fotos / tinyurl.com/
jt6kbtp / Creative Commons CC0

Copyright © 2017 by Cherry Lake Publishing
All rights reserved. No part of this book may be reproduced or
utilized in any form or by any means without written permission
from the publisher.

Library of Congress Cataloging-in-Publication Data
Names: Fontichiaro, Kristin.
Title: Designing boards games / by Kristin Fontichiaro.
Description: Ann Arbor, Michigan : Cherry Lake Publishing, [2017] | Series: Makers
  as Innovators Junior | Series: 21st Century Skills Innovation Library | Includes
  bibliographical references and index. | Audience: Grades: K to Grade 3.
Identifiers: LCCN 2016032424| ISBN 9781634721882 (lib. bdg.) | ISBN
  9781634722544 (pdf) | ISBN 9781634723206 (pbk.) | ISBN 9781634723862 (ebook)
Subjects: LCSH: Board games—Design and construction—Juvenile literature.
Classification: LCC GV1312 .F66 2017 | DDC 794—dc23 LC record available at https://
  lccn.loc.gov/2016032424

Cherry Lake Publishing would like to acknowledge the work of the Partnership for
21st Century Learning. Please visit *www.p21.org* for more information.

Printed in the United States of America
Corporate Graphics

A Note to Adults: Please review the instructions for the activities in this book before allowing children to do them. Be sure to help them with any activities you do not think they can safely complete on their own.

A Note to Kids: Be sure to ask an adult for help with these activities when you need it. Always put your safety first!

Table of Contents

One of the oldest board games in the world is mancala.
Players use rocks or flat marbles.

We Love Board Games

Before TV or the Internet or video games were invented, people played board games. A board game is a game that you play on a board. Some board games have cards. Some have dice. Some have coins, marbles, or secret paths. In this book, you will learn some secrets to creating your own fun board game.

What Will You Need?
1. Game **template** printed from the Web
2. Markers or pens
3. Scrap paper
4. Dice
5. Game pieces

What kind of game would you make if you downloaded this board? This game, called Ludo, has been played for hundreds of years.

Make the Board

One easy way to start making a board game is to use a template. Ask an adult to help you type "board game template" into a search engine like Google or Bing. Click "Images" when the search results come up. Pick a template that looks interesting. Ask an adult to help you print it out. You can also design your own path.

Meet a Game Designer

In 1860, game designer Milton Bradley created his first board game. It is called *The Game of Life*. You can still buy this classic game today. His company was also named Milton Bradley. It continued to release new games long after he died.

You don't need to buy game pieces to make a board game. What can you find around the house?

Kicking Things Off

You need a game piece for each player on the game board. You can use almost anything for a game piece. Pennies, paper clips, rocks, bottle caps, and candies are great choices.

If your board game has a box marked START, put your game pieces there. If there is no START box, write "START" at one end of the path. Write "FINISH" at the other end.

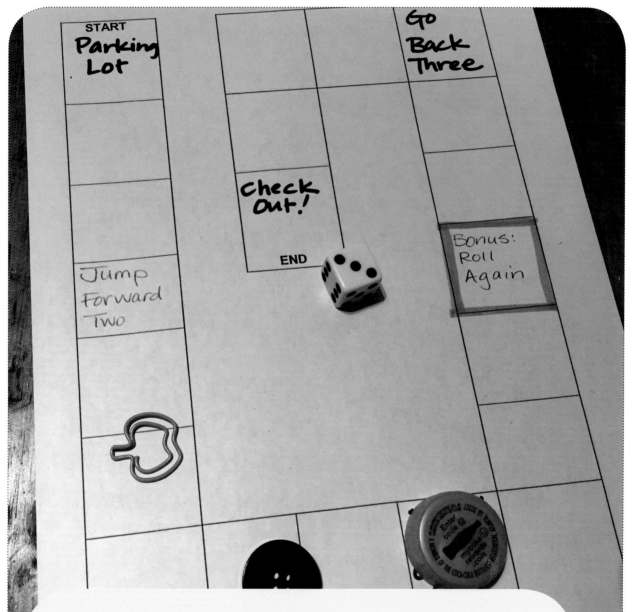

Add a few ideas to your game board that relate to the game's theme. The apple clip and bottle cap show the designer wanted this to be a grocery store game.

Let's Roll!

Roll a die. Move forward the number of spaces on the die. Take turns with your friend.

Wait a minute! Just rolling and moving is boring! Let's add some words to the game path. Words like "Roll again!" or "Move forward five spaces" will help players who land there. Words like "Go back to START" or "Skip a turn" will cause problems for players.

Play your game prototype with friends to test it out.

Test Your Game

Now your board has some good luck squares. It also has some bad luck squares. Time to test the game by playing it! Play for a while. Is the game too hard? Maybe you need to cross out some bad luck squares. Remember that you are making a **prototype**. It is okay to get it messy. You need to make changes to improve your game.

When you play Chutes and Ladders, ladders help you move ahead quickly in the game. Chutes look like playground slides and move you backward in the game.

Challenges Make Games More Fun

All good games have **challenges**. Challenges are events during a game that make it harder to win. In *Chutes and Ladders*, landing on a chute means you slide backward on the game board. In *Monopoly*, you have to give players money when you land on their property. These challenges keep the game from being too easy.

Important Questions Game Designers Ask

1. How does my game start?
2. How does my game end?
3. What challenges will players face?
4. What is the purpose of my game?

You probably only need one die for your game. How does your game change if you roll two dice at once?

Adding Challenges

Talk with your friend. What would make the game more challenging and fun? Rolling an even number to move forward? Using two dice? Do you need more things written on your board? Should you change what is on your board? What makes your game different and better than other games?

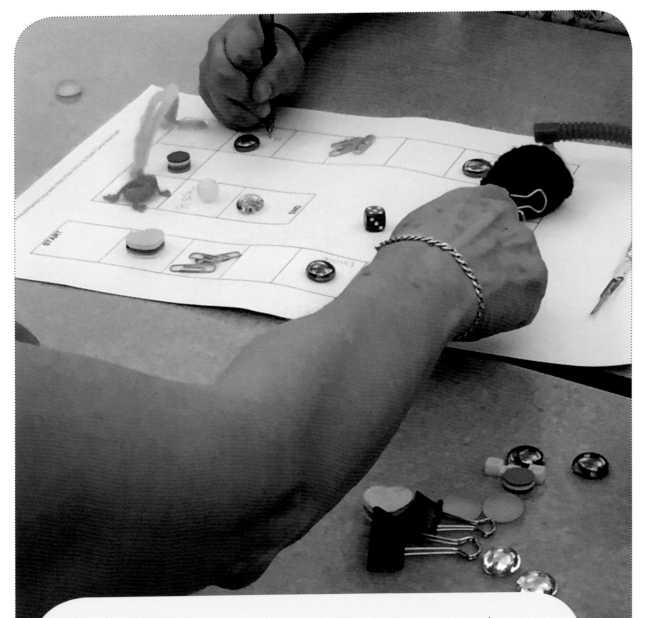

The more you and your friends play, the more you can make your game better.

Every Game Is Unique

Add new things. Play for a while. Test out new **features**. Decide if the things you added make the game better. Keep what works. Get rid of what does not. There are no right or wrong decisions. Playing other games might also give you ideas. Pick and choose features from your favorites. Mix them up to make a brand-new game!

Learning from Other Games

Other games can give you great ideas. Maybe you like how *Candy Land* uses cards. And you love when someone lands on a huge chute in *Chutes and Ladders*. Maybe your game will have some cards and a "Go Back" square to keep it from moving too fast.

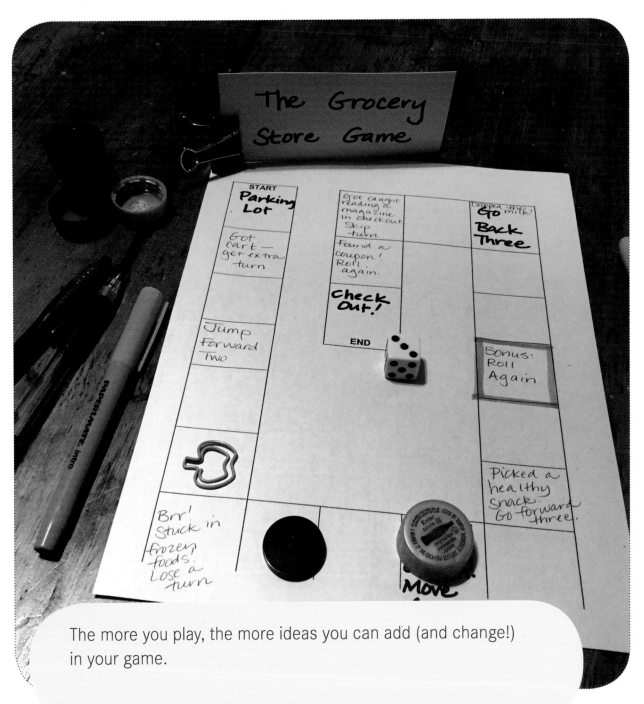

The more you play, the more ideas you can add (and change!) in your game.

Invite Your Friends!

Now your game needs a name. Think of a name that will make people want to try it.

Invite your friends to try your game. Watch them play for a while. Then ask for their **feedback**. Which features made the game more exciting? Would they want to play the game again? Their feedback will help you make your next prototype. Good luck, designers!

Glossary

challenges (CHAL-un-jiz) obstacles you face while playing a game

features (FEE-churz) interesting parts or rules of your game

feedback (FEED-bak) advice you get from other people about your game

prototype (PROH-toh-type) test version of an invention or product

template (TEM-plit) a blank example that can be used as a pattern for creating something

Find Out More

Books

Austic, Greg. *Game Design*. Ann Arbor, MI: Cherry Lake Publishing, 2014.

Cook, Eric. *Prototyping*. Ann Arbor, MI: Cherry Lake Publishing, 2015.

Web Sites

Family Education: Top 10 Classic Board Games for Kids
http://fun.familyeducation.com/slideshow/board-games/48954.html
Learn what board games have been around for decades but are still fun to play with family or friends.

MES English: Free Printables for Teachers—Board Game Templates
www.mes-english.com/games/boardgames.php
Check out these free board games you can print out and play.

Index

About the Author

Kristin Fontichiaro makes things and teaches at the University of Michigan.